MAP PARTS

ALL OVER THE MAP

Kate Torpie

Crabtree Publishing Company
www.crabtreebooks.com

Crabtree Publishing Company

www.crabtreebooks.com

Author: Kate Torpie
Coordinating editor: Chester Fisher
Series editor: Scholastic Ventures
Project editor: Robert Walker
Editor: Reagan Miller
Proofreaders: Molly Aloian, Crystal Sikkens
Production coordinator: Katherine Kantor
Prepress technicians: Katherine Kantor, Ken Wright
Project manager: Santosh Vasudevan (Q2AMEDIA)
Art direction: Rahul Dhiman (Q2AMEDIA
Cover design: Ranjan Singh (Q2AMEDIA)
Design: Dibakar Acharjee (Q2AMEDIA)
Photo research: Sejal Sehgal Wani (Q2AMEDIA)

Photographs:
Cia.gov: p. 18
Dreamstime: Indiansummer: p. 19; Megumi: p. 21 (top)
Fotolia: Profotokris: p. 6 (top right), 30 (top right); Titimel35:
   p. 21 (bottom); Thor Jorgen Udvang: p. 30 (bottom right)
Istockphoto: Jakub Semeniuk: p. 1, 20
Jupiter Images: Imageshop: p. 11 (globe)
Map Resources: p. 28–29
NASA: p. 4, 25 (top)
Nationalatlas.gov: p. 12, 14, 15, 16–17, 31 (top right)
Shutterstock: Stasys Eidiejus: p. 22–23, 31 (top left); Cindy Hughes:
   cover (bottom right); Gabriel Moisa: cover (background)
   Pavel Losevsky: p. 5, 30 (top left); Noah Strycker: p. 26
United States Federal Government: p. 1 (background), 24–25, 31 (bottom)
Usgs.gov: cover (background)

Illustrations:
Q2AMedia

Library and Archives Canada Cataloguing in Publication

Torpie, Kate, 1974-
   Map parts / Kate Torpie.

(All over the map)
Includes index.
ISBN 978-0-7787-4268-5 (bound).--ISBN 978-0-7787-4273-9 (pbk.)

   1. Map reading--Juvenile literature. 2. Maps--Juvenile literature.
I. Title. II. Series: All over the map (St. Catharines, Ont.)

GA105.6.T67 2008   j912.01'4   C2008-903495-3

Library of Congress Cataloging-in-Publication Data

Torpie, Kate, 1974-
   Map parts / Kate Torpie.
      p. cm. -- (All over the map)
   Includes index.
   ISBN-13: 978-0-7787-4273-9 (pbk. : alk. paper)
   ISBN-10: 0-7787-4273-3 (pbk. : alk. paper)
   ISBN-13: 978-0-7787-4268-5 (reinforced library binding : alk. paper)
   ISBN-10: 0-7787-4268-7 (reinforced library binding : alk. paper)
   1. Maps--Juvenile literature. I. Title. II. Series.

GA105.6.T669 2009
912--dc22
                                    2008023526

Crabtree Publishing Company

www.crabtreebooks.com   1-800-387-7650

Published in Canada
Crabtree Publishing
616 Welland Ave.
St. Catharines, Ontario
L2M 5V6

Published in the United States
Crabtree Publishing
PMB16A
350 Fifth Ave., Suite 3308
New York, NY 10118

Published in the United Kingdom
Crabtree Publishing
White Cross Mills
High Town, Lancaster
LA1 4XS

Published in Australia
Crabtree Publishing
386 Mt. Alexander Rd.
Ascot Vale (Melbourne)
VIC 3032

CONTENTS

Where in the World Am I?

At My House! 4

In My City! 8

In My State! 12

In My Country! 16

Here on Earth! 20

Finding Your Way in the World 26

So Here I Am! 30

Glossary and Index 32

Where in the World Am I?
At My House!

Hello, my name is Max. Today in school, I learned about **maps**. A map is a representation of a place. People draw maps or print them on paper. Maps are tools to help us find where we are and where we are going. Now that I learned about maps, I can tell you exactly where I am!

▲ *I live on planet Earth. So do you! That doesn't mean we are in the same place. Where exactly on Earth am I?*

▲ *I am in my bedroom. This is a picture of my bedroom.*
I decorated it myself. But where exactly is my bedroom?

The parts of a map help us understand how to read the information.

All maps have **titles**. Titles tell you what the map will show you. This map is called "My House." That's because the map will show you where all the rooms in my house are!

▲ *This is the house where I live.*

MY HOUSE

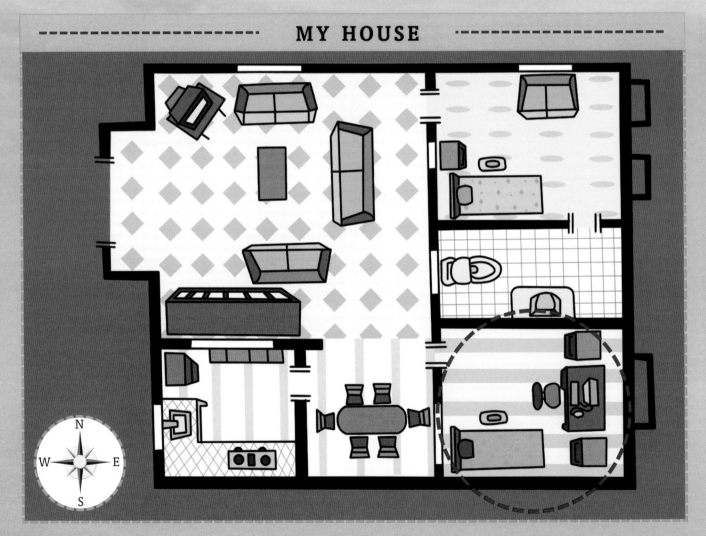

▲ *Here is my room.*

A **compass rose** is a part on a map. The compass rose is used to show the positions of north, south, east, and west. It is usually placed in the lower left-hand corner of a map. The compass rose is used to locate places on a map using direction.

My house is in a neighborhood near the park and the beach. Look at the map below. The park is east of my neighborhood.

Can you find my neighborhood? Use the compass rose to help you find the direction east. Can you see the park east of my neighborhood?

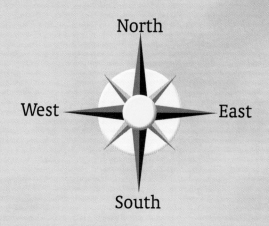

This is a large compass rose. Can you find two smaller ones on these two pages?

MY NEIGHBORHOOD

My neighborhood

Where is my neighborhood in this map? Where is the compass rose?

Where in the World Am I?
In My City!

My neighborhood is exactly in the city of Long Beach, New York. I'll try to draw a map of the busy part of my city to show you. First, I'll title it: The Busy Section of Long Beach, NY.

You can see all the places that matter most to me on this map. I labeled my house, my school, my favorite stores, and our two main streets. They sure took a long time to draw!

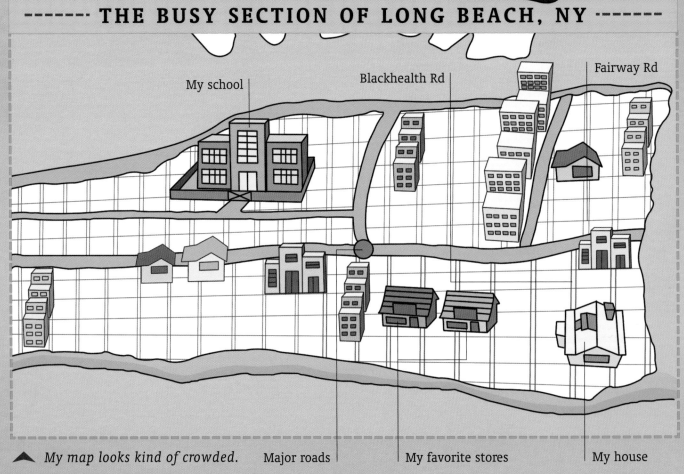

------- **THE BUSY SECTION OF LONG BEACH, NY** -------

My school | Blackhealth Rd | Fairway Rd

▲ *My map looks kind of crowded.*　　Major roads　　My favorite stores　　My house

8

This map shows the same information that my drawing did. It's a lot easier to read! That's because they used **symbols** and a **legend** instead of labeling all the places. A map has a legend to explain the meaning of each symbol used on the map. If a map has a symbol on it, it needs to have a legend. These two map parts go together.

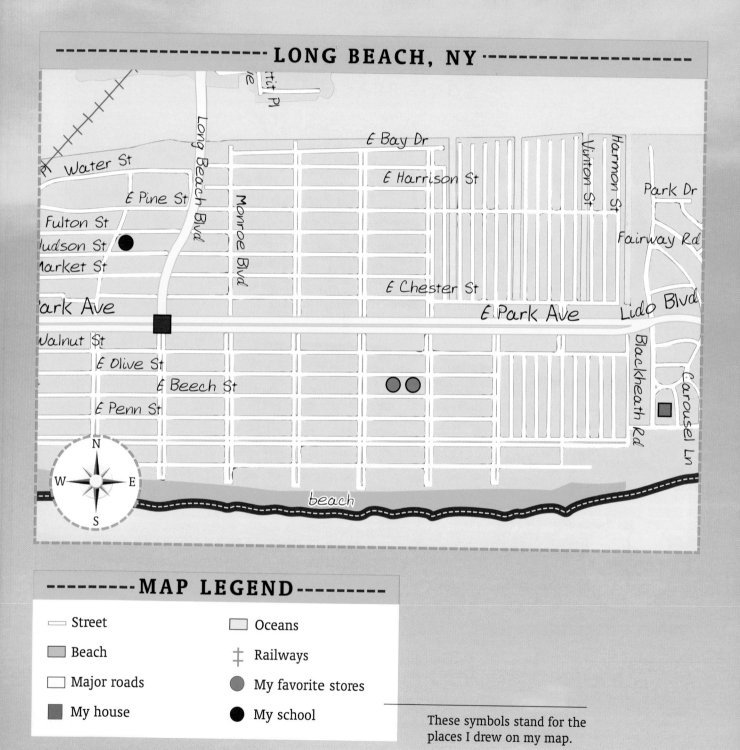

----------- **LONG BEACH, NY** -----------

Water St
E Pine St
Fulton St
Hudson St
Market St
Park Ave
Walnut St
E Olive St
E Beech St
E Penn St
Long Beach Blvd
Monroe Blvd
tit Pl
E Bay Dr
E Harrison St
E Chester St
E Park Ave
Vinton St
Harmon St
Park Dr
Fairway Rd
Lido Blvd
Blackheath Rd
Carousel Ln
beach

N W E S

--------- **MAP LEGEND** ---------

⬭ Street		☐ Oceans	
▣ Beach		‡ Railways	
☐ Major roads		⬤ My favorite stores	
▪ My house		● My school	

These symbols stand for the places I drew on my map.

9

Where in the World Am I? In My State!

Look at this map, titled "New York Counties" to see exactly where New York City is.

Places are outlined to show their **boundaries**. A boundary is a border that separates one place from another. This map shows the boundaries for each county. New York City is in Kings County. Long Beach is in Nassau County.

MAP LEGEND

—— State Border

--- Country Border

▭ Lakes and Rivers

▭ Oceans

▭ Other States

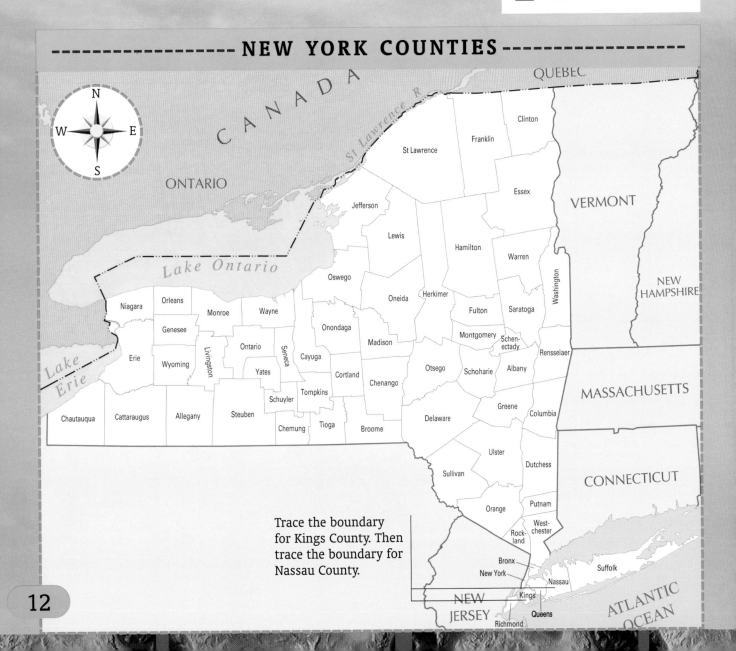

NEW YORK COUNTIES

Trace the boundary for Kings County. Then trace the boundary for Nassau County.

----- NASSAU COUNTY -----

Miles
0   2

25A   NORTHERN BLVD.   Old Westbury

LONG ISLAND EXPWY.

NORTHERN STATE PKWY.

495

25   **NASSAU**

MEADOWBROOK STATE PKWY.

QUEENS   SOUTHERN STATE PKWY.   TOWN OF HEMPSTEAD

Rockville Centre   Merrick

27   SUNRISE HWY.   Freeport

LOOP STATE PKWY.

Long Beach   LIDO BLVD.

JONES BEACH

Atlantic Beach   Lido Beach

Atlantic Ocean

N
W   E
S

▲ *This map shows only one county of New York. Do you remember where Nassau County is on page 12?*

Here is another map, titled "Nassau County." Some map parts, such as compass roses, always look the same. Look at other map parts and see how they are different.

This map shows a smaller area than the map on page 12. Places were drawn larger. The scale gives you a larger view of the area. So this is a **large scale map**.

The map on page 12 is a **small scale map**. It shows a larger area. The scale makes the area look smaller.

> If the map shows a big area, it is small scale. If a map shows a small area, it is large scale.

13

Here's another map of New York State. The title is "Highways in New York State." This map shows different information than the county map of New York State. Both of the maps may show the same state, but the information about the state is different from map to map.

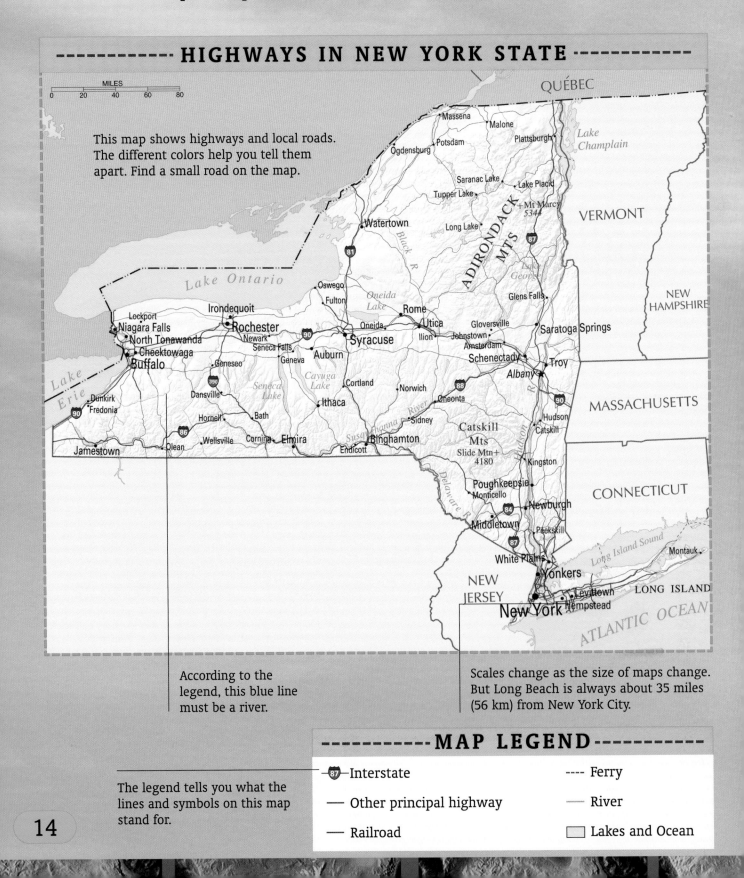

HIGHWAYS IN NEW YORK STATE

MILES
0   20   40   60   80

This map shows highways and local roads. The different colors help you tell them apart. Find a small road on the map.

QUÉBEC

Massena
Malone
Ogdensburg   Potsdam   Plattsburgh   Lake Champlain
Saranac Lake   Lake Placid
Tupper Lake   +Mt Marcy 5344   VERMONT
Watertown   Long Lake   ADIRONDACK MTS   Lake George
NEW HAMPSHIRE
Oswego   Glens Falls
Fulton   Oneida Lake   Rome
Irondequoit   Gloversville   Saratoga Springs
Lockport   Oneida   Utica   Johnstown
Niagara Falls   Rochester   Newark   Syracuse   Ilion   Amsterdam   Schenectady   Troy
North Tonawanda   Seneca Falls   Auburn   Albany
Cheektowaga   Geneva   Schenectady
Buffalo   Geneseo   Cayuga Lake   Cortland   Norwich   Hudson   MASSACHUSETTS
Lake Erie   Seneca Lake   Ithaca   Oneonta   Catskill
Dansville   Sidney   Catskill Mts
Dunkirk   Hornell   Bath   Slide Mtn+ 4180   Kingston
Fredonia   Wellsville   Corning   Elmira   Binghamton   Poughkeepsie
Jamestown   Olean   Endicott   Monticello   CONNECTICUT
Middletown   Newburgh
White Plains   Peekskill
Long Island Sound   Montauk
NEW JERSEY   Yonkers   LONG ISLAND
New York   Levittown   Hempstead   ATLANTIC OCEAN

Black R.
Susquehanna River
Delaware R.
Hudson R.

According to the legend, this blue line must be a river.

Scales change as the size of maps change. But Long Beach is always about 35 miles (56 km) from New York City.

MAP LEGEND

The legend tells you what the lines and symbols on this map stand for.

—87—Interstate

—— Other principal highway

— Railroad

---- Ferry

— River

☐ Lakes and Ocean

14

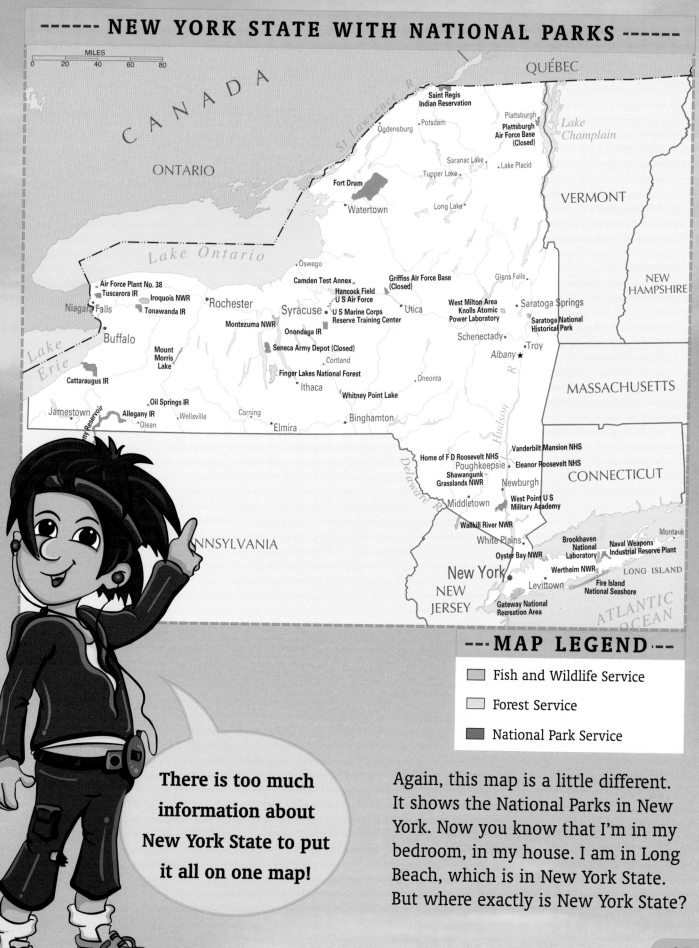

MILES
0   20   40   60   80

QUÉBEC

CANADA

ONTARIO

Saint Regis
Indian Reservation

Ogdensburg • Potsdam

Plattsburgh

Plattsburgh
Air Force Base
(Closed)

Lake
Champlain

Saranac Lake

Tupper Lake •   • Lake Placid

Fort Drum

VERMONT

Watertown

Long Lake •

Lake Ontario

NEW
HAMPSHIRE

• Oswego

Air Force Plant No. 38
Tuscarora IR

Iroquois NWR

Tonawanda IR

Niagara Falls

Camden Test Annex

Hancock Field
U S Air Force

Griffiss Air Force Base
(Closed)

Glens Falls •

Saratoga Springs

Rochester

Syracuse

U S Marine Corps
Reserve Training Center

Utica

West Milton Area
Knolls Atomic
Power Laboratory

Saratoga National
Historical Park

Montezuma NWR

Onondaga IR

Schenectady

Buffalo

Lake
Erie

Mount
Morris
Lake

Seneca Army Depot (Closed)

Troy

Albany ★

Cortland

MASSACHUSETTS

Cattaraugus IR

Finger Lakes National Forest

Ithaca

Oneonta •

Oil Springs IR

Whitney Point Lake

Jamestown

Reservoir

Allegany IR

Wellsville

Corning

Elmira

Binghamton

Olean

Vanderbilt Mansion NHS

Home of F D Roosevelt NHS

Poughkeepsie

Eleanor Roosevelt NHS

Shawangunk
Grasslands NWR

Newburgh

CONNECTICUT

PNNSYLVANIA

Middletown

West Point U S
Military Academy

Wallkill River NWR

White Plains •

Montauk

Brookhaven
National
Laboratory

Naval Weapons
Industrial Reserve Plant

Oyster Bay NWR

Wertheim NWR

LONG ISLAND

New York

Levittown

Fire Island
National Seashore

NEW
JERSEY

Gateway National
Recreation Area

ATLANTIC
OCEAN

--- MAP LEGEND ---

- Fish and Wildlife Service
- Forest Service
- National Park Service

There is too much information about New York State to put it all on one map!

Again, this map is a little different. It shows the National Parks in New York. Now you know that I'm in my bedroom, in my house. I am in Long Beach, which is in New York State. But where exactly is New York State?

Where in the World Am I?
In My Country!

THE UNITED STATES

CANADA

Lake of the Woods

WASHINGTON
Seattle
Spokane
Olympia
Portland
Salem
Eugene
OREGON

MONTANA
Missoula
Helena
Butte
Billings

NORTH DAKOTA
Grand Forks
Bismarck
Fargo

Duluth
MINNESOTA
Minneapolis
St Paul

Lake Superior
MICHIGAN

WISCONSIN
Green Bay
Milwaukee
Madison
Grand Rapids
Lansing

Boise
IDAHO
Pocatello

WYOMING
Casper

SOUTH DAKOTA
Rapid City
Pierre
Sioux Falls

Sioux City
IOWA
Des Moines
Cedar Rapids

Chicago
Toledo

NEVADA
Reno
Carson City

GREAT
SALT
LAKE
Salt Lake City
Provo

Cheyenne
Fort Collins

NEBRASKA
Omaha
Lincoln

Peoria
ILLINOIS
Springfield
INDIANA
Indianapolis
Fort Wayne

San Francisco
Oakland
San Jose
Sacramento
CALIFORNIA
Fresno

UTAH

Denver
COLORADO
Pueblo

Kansas City
Topeka
Kansas City
MISSOURI
Jefferson City
St Louis

Evansville
Louisville
KENTUCKY

GREAT
BASIN

Las Vegas
Bakersfield
Los Angeles
San Bernardino
San Diego

Flagstaff
ARIZONA
Phoenix
Tucson

Santa Fe
Albuquerque
NEW MEXICO
Roswell

Amarillo
Lubbock

KANSAS
Wichita

OKLAHOMA
Oklahoma City
Tulsa
Fort Smith

Springfield
ARKANSAS
Little Rock

Nashville
TENNESSEE
Memphis

PACIFIC OCEAN

El Paso

Fort Worth
Dallas
TEXAS
Austin
San Antonio
Houston

Shreveport
MISSISSIPPI
Jackson
Meridian

LOUISIANA
Baton Rouge
New Orleans
Biloxi
Mobile

Birmingham
ALABAMA
Montgomery

GULF OF MEXICO

MEXICO

HAWAII
Honolulu
Hilo
PACIFIC OCEAN

0   100 mi
0   100 km

ARCTIC OCEAN
RUSSIA

BROOKS RANGE
ALASKA
Fairbanks
ALASKA RANGE
Anchorage
Yukon
CANADA
Juneau
GULF OF ALASKA
BERING SEA
PACIFIC OCEAN

0   200 mi
0   200 km

Albers equal area projection
0   100   200   300 mi
0   100   200   300 km

New York State is one of the United States. This map is called "The United States." It is a small scale map. It shows each of the states in our country, and gives you an idea about the shape of the land. Can you find where in the United States New York is exactly? Can you find your state?

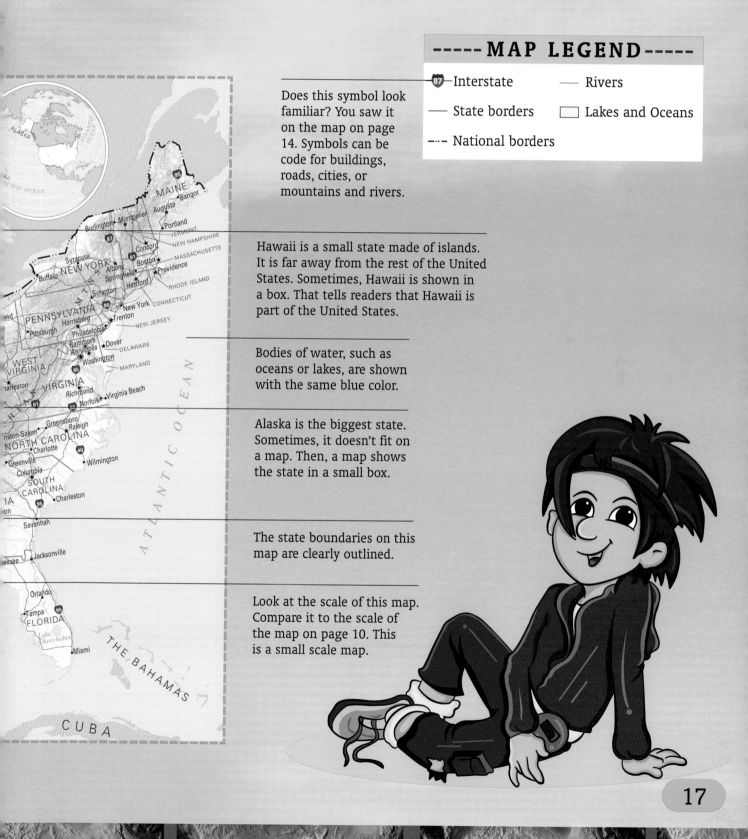

----- MAP LEGEND -----

🛡87 Interstate — Rivers

— State borders ☐ Lakes and Oceans

-·-· National borders

Does this symbol look familiar? You saw it on the map on page 14. Symbols can be code for buildings, roads, cities, or mountains and rivers.

Hawaii is a small state made of islands. It is far away from the rest of the United States. Sometimes, Hawaii is shown in a box. That tells readers that Hawaii is part of the United States.

Bodies of water, such as oceans or lakes, are shown with the same blue color.

Alaska is the biggest state. Sometimes, it doesn't fit on a map. Then, a map shows the state in a small box.

The state boundaries on this map are clearly outlined.

Look at the scale of this map. Compare it to the scale of the map on page 10. This is a small scale map.

Like the last map, this map shows the United States.
But this one gives you different information. It shows
the countries that border the United States.

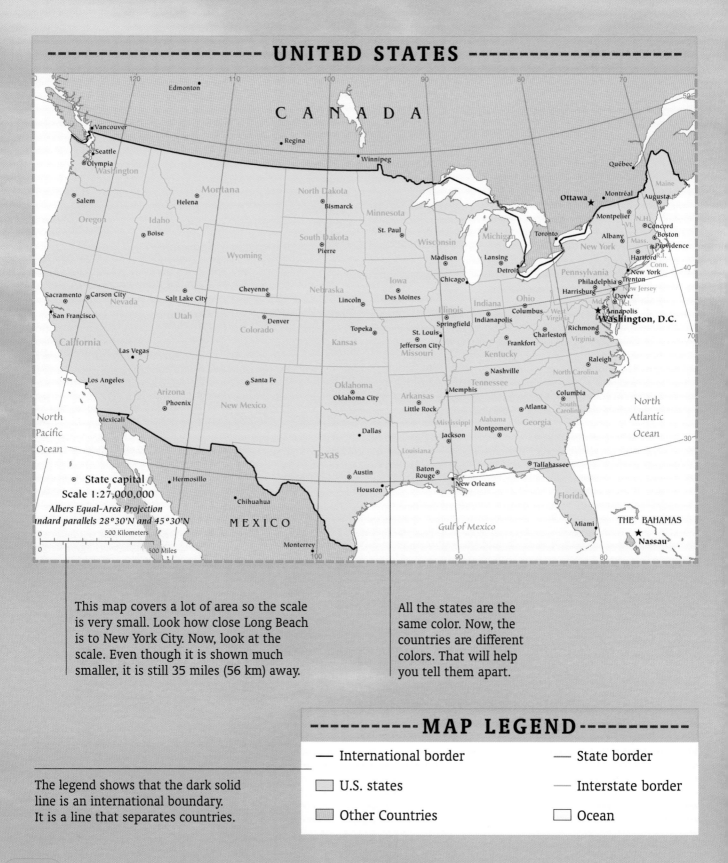

UNITED STATES

This map covers a lot of area so the scale
is very small. Look how close Long Beach
is to New York City. Now, look at the
scale. Even though it is shown much
smaller, it is still 35 miles (56 km) away.

All the states are the
same color. Now, the
countries are different
colors. That will help
you tell them apart.

The legend shows that the dark solid
line is an international boundary.
It is a line that separates countries.

---------- **MAP LEGEND** ----------

— International border   — State border

☐ U.S. states   — Interstate border

☐ Other Countries   ☐ Ocean

The map below shows more of Mexico and Canada. Read the map title. Now we know what the map is showing us: the continent of North America.

So, now you know where I am! I'm in my bedroom, in my house, in my neighborhood, in my city, in my state, in the United States, on the continent of North America! But where exactly is North America?

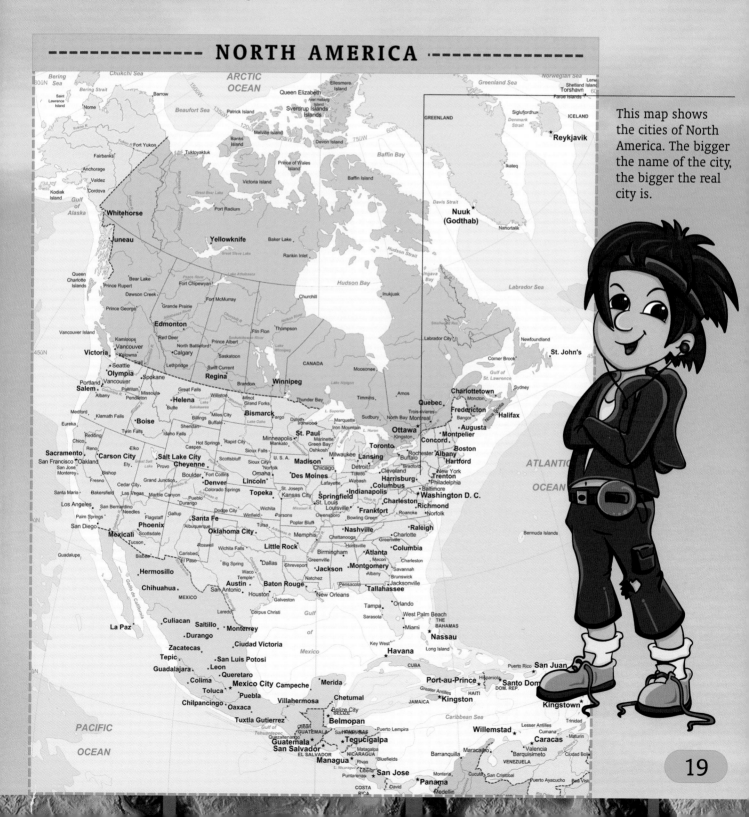

NORTH AMERICA

This map shows the cities of North America. The bigger the name of the city, the bigger the real city is.

Where in the World Am I?
Here on Earth!

North America is a continent on Earth. The world is not flat—you know that. But maps ARE flat. Maps are like opened **globes**. If you peeled the picture off a globe, and tried to lay it flat, you would have a map.

▶ *A globe is a map, but it shows the whole world in its round form. Globes can be based on pictures of Earth, so they can be made exactly right. But you can't make a round ball on flat paper.*

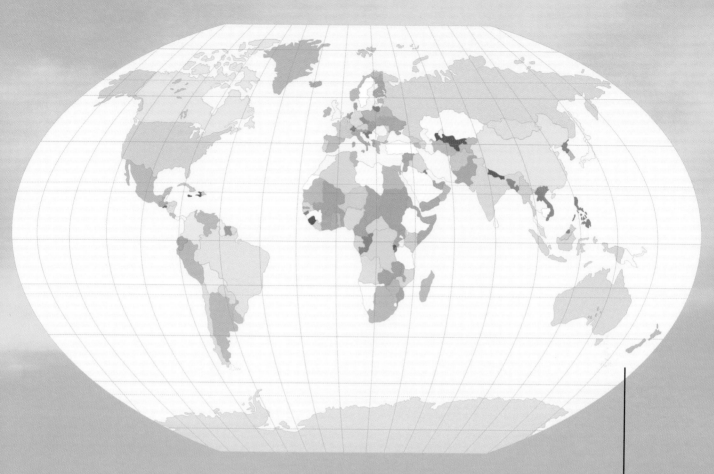

Maps made this way are very popular. They are called **projection maps**.

Projection maps are not always perfect. There are some mistakes in how big or where continents are. For example, this projection map cuts off part of Antarctica. It also makes Alaska and Russia look far apart. They are really close together!

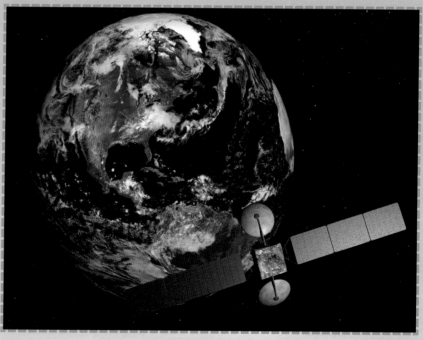

Globes are shaped like a ball because Earth is shaped like a ball.

Map Facts

No one knew that America existed when Columbus traveled here in 1492. He thought he had sailed to India.

The United States is a country in North America. You can see the continent below. Like small maps, this big map has a title: "Map of the World." That title tells you that this map will show you the location of the countries in the world.

World maps show lines that go all around Earth. Those are lines of **latitude**. The center line is the **equator**. The lines aren't really on Earth.

MAP OF THE WORLD

They just help people measure where places are. Each latitude line is a measure of how far north or south a place is from the equator.

World maps show lines going up and down Earth. Those are lines of **longitude**. Just like lines of latitude aren't really on Earth, neither are the lines of longitude. They tell how far east or west a place is.

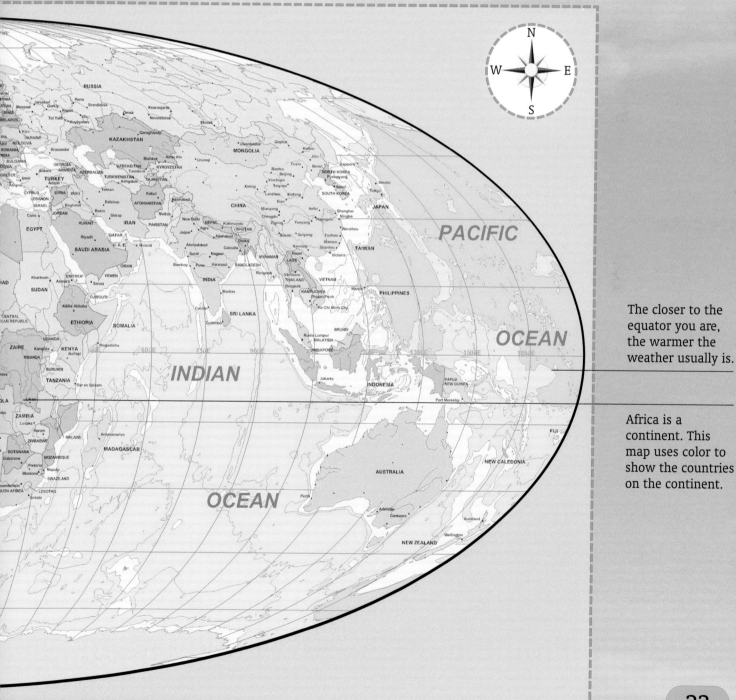

The closer to the equator you are, the warmer the weather usually is.

Africa is a continent. This map uses color to show the countries on the continent.

This is another world map, but its title is different:
"Physical Map of the World." A **physical map** is a
map that shows natural features, such as
mountains, lakes, and rivers.

PHYSICAL MAP OF THE WORLD

Scale 1:35,000,000

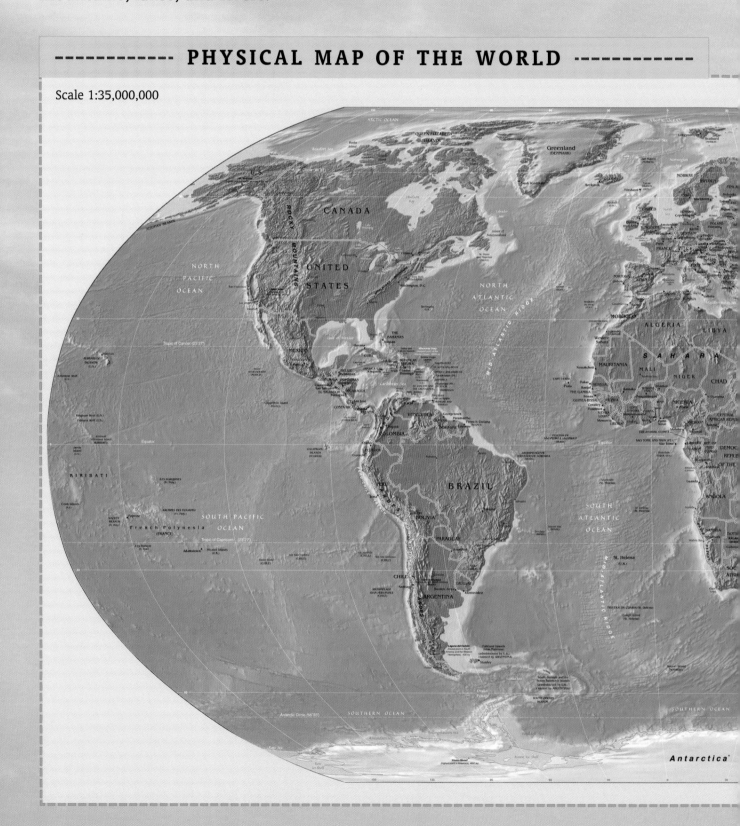

Map Facts

There is land under the oceans, too. This is called the Mariana Trench. It is deeper than any other part of any ocean!

As the color on the land changes from green to tan, the land goes from flat to hilly. The colors on the land get lighter as the land turns into mountains.

Now, Africa's countries are not different colors. That's because this map doesn't show countries— it shows the shape of the land.

Even though this map uses color, the bodies of water are still blue. Water is blue on nearly all maps.

Finding Your Way in the World

No matter what a map tells you, all maps have some of the same map parts. They all have:
- a title to tell you what the map is about,
- a compass rose to tell you which way is north,
- a scale to show you how to read distance, and
- a legend to show you what each symbol means.

▼ *This is a picture of my classroom! But where is my desk?*

Well, let's look at these maps. Here is a map I made of my school campus. I think I will call it "West School Campus." Even though it is just a handmade map, it has all the parts that you need to read it.

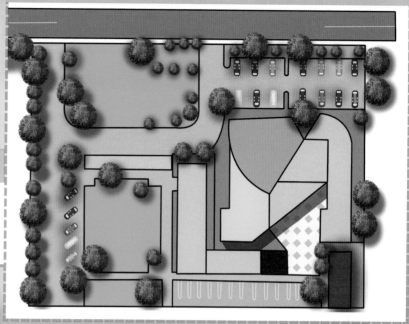

WEST SCHOOL CAMPUS

--- MAP LEGEND ---

▨	Playground / Lawn	▨	Library
▨	Classes	■	Cafeteria
▨	Administration	▨	Gym

The legend shows where the playground, library, cafeteria, and gym are. Can you find each?

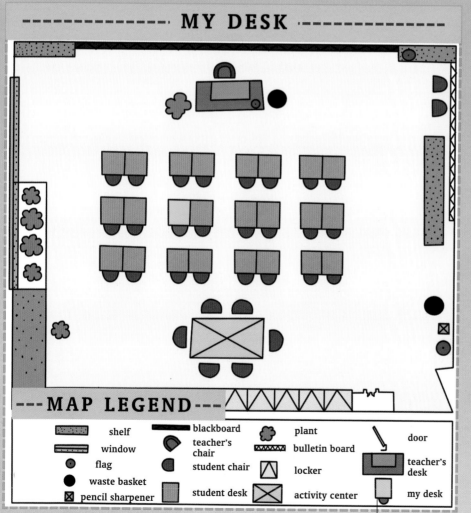

MY DESK

--- MAP LEGEND ---

▨	shelf	▬	blackboard	✿	plant	╲	door
▭	window	◥	teacher's chair	∿∿∿	bulletin board		
◉	flag	◖	student chair	▨	locker	▭	teacher's desk
●	waste basket						
⊠	pencil sharpener	▨	student desk	⊠	activity center	▢	my desk

▲ *The title of this map is "My Desk." Now you know why you would use it. If you wanted to find my desk in a classroom of desks, this map would help you! I drew this map myself.*

The legend shows you a symbol for my desk. Can you find it?

The two maps on this page are very different.
But they both show Long Island!

Both maps have compass roses, titles, and symbols.
Once you know your map parts, you will be able to
read any map—no matter what it's trying to tell you.

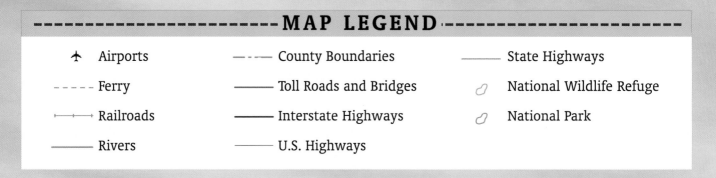

MAP LEGEND

- ✈ Airports
- – – – – Ferry
- ⊢•——→ Railroads
- ——— Rivers
- –•–•– County Boundaries
- ——— Toll Roads and Bridges
- ——— Interstate Highways
- ——— U.S. Highways
- ——— State Highways
- ⬭ National Wildlife Refuge
- ⬭ National Park

LONG ISLAND MAP FOR TOURISTS

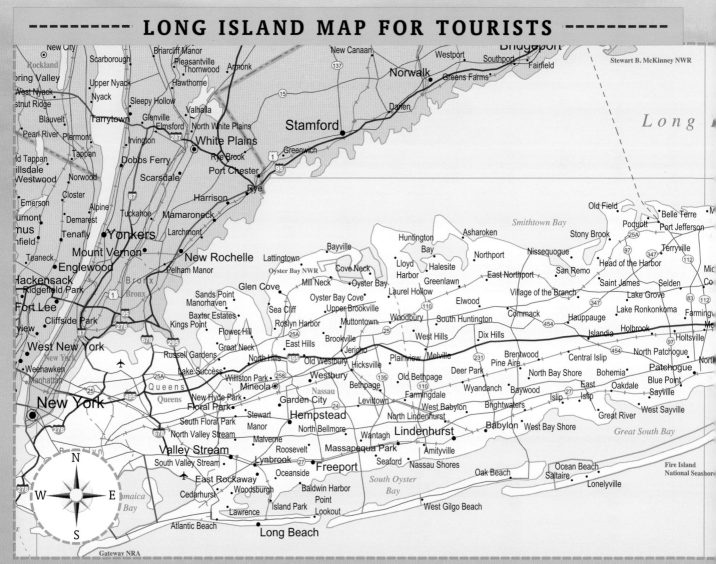

▲ *The title of this map is "Long Island Map for Tourists." Look
at the legend. There are symbols for roads, ferries, and trains.
This map must tell people how to get around Long Island.*

LIGHTHOUSES OF LONG ISLAND

Long Island
Sound

Atlantic Ocean

▲ The title of this map is "Lighthouses of Long Island."
It doesn't show any roads. There is only one symbol
on this map—a lighthouse! That's all this map shows.

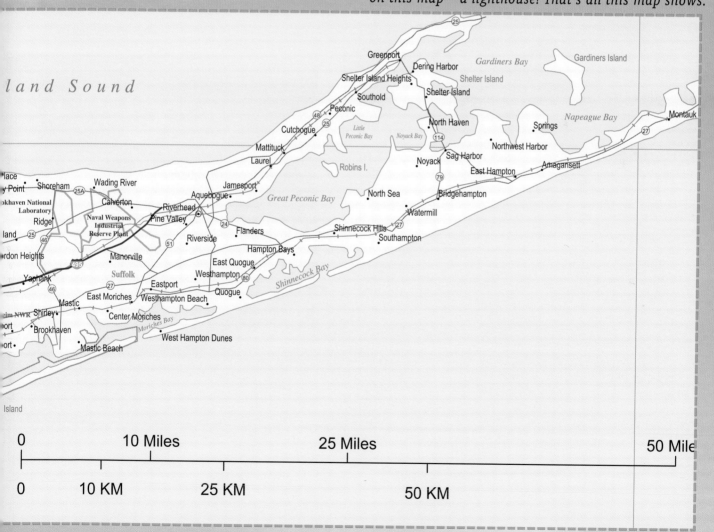

So Here I Am!

Okay, so NOW do you
know where I am?

▲ In my house...

▲ I am in my bedroom...

▲ In my neighborhood...

▲ In my city called Long Beach...

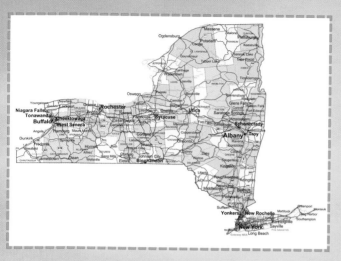

▲ *In my state called New York...*

▲ *In the country called The United States...*

Map Facts

Long ago, people sailed across oceans without maps. They watched the birds and stars to figure out where they were. When they came home, they made maps. Some are very exact.

▲ *On the continent called North America and on the planet called EARTH!*

Where in the world are YOU?

Glossary

boundaries Lines that show where one place ends and another begins

compass rose A map part that shows you which way on the map is north, south, east, and west

equator The line of latitude that circles the center of Earth from east to west

large scale map A map that shows a small area of land

latitude Lines on maps that are used to measure how far a place is from the equator

legend A key to decoding symbols on a map

longitude Lines on maps that are used to measure how far east or west a place is

scale A map part that shows you how to read distance on a map

small scale map A map that shows a large area of land

symbol A shape or color that represents a building, place, or other part on a map

title A map part that tells you what the map will show you

Index

boundary 12, 17, 18

compass rose 7, 10, 13, 26, 28

equator 22, 23

latitude 22, 23

legend 9, 10, 12, 14, 15, 17, 18, 26, 27, 28

longitude 23

physical map 24

Mariana Trench 25

scale 10, 11, 13, 14, 17, 18, 24, 26

symbol 9, 10, 14, 17, 26, 27, 28, 29

title 6, 8, 10, 12, 13, 14, 19, 22, 24, 26, 27, 28, 29

Printed in the U.S.A. - CG